YOUR KNOWLEDGE HAS VALUE

Unlocking Retail Success. Leveraging Analytics Stack Solutions for Data-Driven Decision-Making and Competitive Edge

Olalekan Olaniru

Bibliographic information published by the German National Library:

The German National Library lists this publication in the National Bibliography; detailed bibliographic data are available on the Internet at http://dnb.dnb.de.

ISBN: 9783346994035
This book is also available as an ebook.

© GRIN Publishing GmbH
Trappentreustraße 1
80339 München

Print and binding: Books on Demand GmbH, Norderstedt, Germany
Printed on acid-free paper from responsible sources.

The present work has been carefully prepared. Nevertheless, authors and publishers do not incur liability for the correctness of information, notes, links and advice as well as any printing errors.

GRIN web shop: https://www.grin.com/document/1437849

Comparative Study of Cloud-Based Vs On-Premises Analytics Stack for Retail Business

Olalekan Ebenezer Olaniru

January 7th 2024

Table of Contents

List of figures

List of Tables

1 Introduction

The amount of data generated by the retail sector is constantly growing, and the old way of using manual data management solutions can no longer handle it. The Home Depot, a multinational home improvement retail firm, is one example of a company in this sector, and other retail firms that generates huge amount of data includes the sales department of the fast-moving consumer goods companies such as Procter & Gamble, Coca-Cola, Nestlé, PepsiCo, and Unilever. These companies sell wide variety of products characterized by constant high demand and deliver them to thousands of retailers or stores spread across numerous locations. According to a Harvard Business Review, collecting customer data and utilizing it to improve goods and services is a tried-and-true tactic, but historically the method was cumbersome, time-consuming, and had a narrow reach (Hagiu, Wright, 2020). A recent survey of 179 publicly traded firms showed that companies that adopted a data-driven decision-making approach have higher profitability, market value, and productivity that is 5 – 6 % higher than others (Bryanjolfsson, Hitt, Kim, 2011). This study explores the challenges and opportunities of implementing an analytics stack solution for a traditional retail company that seeks to enhance its data-driven decision-making, productivity, and competitive advantage.

The analytics stack solution is designed to enable real-time tracking of retail sales across various channels, including physical stores, e-commerce, wholesale, and others, to capture the complex and dynamic consumer behavior in the retail industry. Analytics stack brings digitization to retail for better productivity. For instance, in physical stores, the model will relieve salespeople from administrative tasks, allowing them more time for actual sales and providing management with quick, precise, and comprehensive sales feedback critical for decision-making (Wedell, Hempeck, 1987). Traditional stores and e-commerce are not independent of one another but are complementary channels in an omnichannel ecosystem. By utilizing data on what, where, how many, and how frequently customers buy a specific product based on availability, opportunity exists to broadcast real-time marketing messages to customers' smartphones when shopping close to a targeted product (Microsoft, 2022).

Data from various point-of-sale systems, social media platforms, and e-commerce platforms must be continuously gathered, stored, and analyzed in real-time to help decision-makers in the retail sector stay competitive. Adopting business applications like Distributor Management Systems (DMS), Enterprise Resource Planning (ERP), and Customer Relationship Management (CRM) and combining them into an analytics stack can make this achievable. The organization becomes incredibly versatile as a result of the crucial insights that data generated at every level of the value chain delivers, and it aids in implementing a data-driven decision-making approach for increased efficiency and profitability (Bryanjolfsson, Hitt, Kim, 2011). The unstructured data (e.g., customer review) will be organized, processed, and then analyzed by an analytics stack to yield insightful results.

This study aims to explore whether deploying the solutions on-premises or using cloud services is the optimum method for integrating the sales data gathered at various retail touchpoints in an analytics stack. Other things to explore in this study are the factors to consider before making this decision: data type, volume, and data security required in the retail industry, as well as data privacy, flexibility, and scaling options. In addition, we will consider the change management decisions and the key components that make up a retail analytics stack.

2.1 Overview of On-Premises and Cloud Solutions

The analytics stack requires identifying and connecting various systems and software to enable data collection, storage, processing, analysis, and visualization, as depicted in Figure 1. The deployment decision between on-premises and cloud-based solutions is crucial in any analytics project, and it can be challenging at times because they both offer advantages and disadvantages. However, in the retail sector, it is crucial to think about a solution that meets the majority need of the business such as inventory management, real-time sales capture, and demand forecasting. The concepts behind on-premises and cloud solutions, as well as other important considerations, are covered in this section.

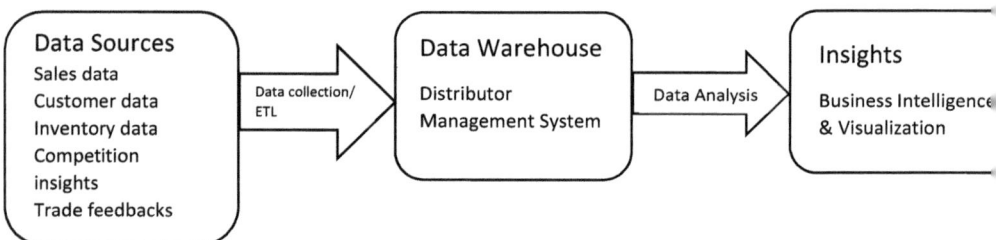

Figure 1: Key Components of Analytics Stack Showing Various Data Sources That Can Be Integrated into A Data Warehouse Where Business Insights Can Be Obtained

With an on-premises solution, the business is totally in control because every step, from implementation to usage, is carried out internally at a physical location with no involvement from outside parties. Servers and server rooms, software, platforms, hardware, and infrastructure (including communications, storage, backup, and many more), are situated inside the organization's physical boundaries (Kanade, 2021). The company also takes responsibility for software installation, database, maintenance, safety, and upgrades. It is important to consider the following advantages and disadvantages in making a decision about whether on-premises solution is the right choice for the organization's analytics stack (Kanade, 2021).

1. Total Cost of Ownership (TCO): With a one-time user license payment, an on-premises solution may have a potentially lower TCO compared to other options.
2. Control: The company retains control over the data, hardware, and software platforms, which can be advantageous for organizations with specific security or compliance requirements.

2

3. Uptime: On-premises solutions can be accessed without relying on an internet connection, ensuring uninterrupted access to the analytics stack.

However, it is essential to consider the potential drawbacks of an on-premises solution, which include:

1. High cost of setup, maintenance, and upgrades: Implementing and maintaining an on-premises solution often involves significant upfront costs, ongoing expenses for system upkeep, and investments for future upgrades.
2. Requires high technical resources: Adequate technical resources, such as a skilled team for data backups and disaster recovery, are necessary to manage an on-premises solution effectively.

Cloud computing, on the other hand, can be defined as the on-demand availability of computer system resources, particularly data storage and processing, without direct active supervision of the user (Zawaideh et al., 2022). The goal of cloud computing is to provide particular system resources as needed. Numerous cutting-edge discoveries served as inspiration for the idea of cloud computing, which shares some traits with earlier computer models. Cloud computing has important financial and performance advantages over conventional methods, which are essential for the retail sector to stay competitive.

The traditional cloud computing paradigm has three service tiers depending on the user's needs. Software as a service (SaaS) provides online, on-demand access to software applications. Platform as a Service (PaaS) offers a computing platform and environment for users to create internet-enabled applications and services. Over the internet, infrastructure as a service (IaaS) provides computational resources (servers, storage, and virtualization). With its lower costs, on-demand services, scalability, and service elasticity, cloud computing has completely changed how small, medium-sized, and large-scale businesses conduct business. These advantages make many companies adopt cloud services, which leads to growth in the demand for cloud service providers (CSPs) such as Amazon Web Services (AWS), Google Cloud, IBM, Microsoft Azure, Oracle, SAP, and many more (Tomar et al., 2022).

Because CSPs offer different performance options, it can be difficult for cloud customers to choose the best solution to satisfy their functional and non-functional needs. A variety of variables affect the decision on which service to choose. To select the best cloud service, a cloud user must ascertain the service requirements for Quality of Service (QoS) (Tomar et al., 2022). For instance, it is crucial to establish service characteristics using performance or reliability requirements. On the other hand, cloud consumers also place a high value on privacy and convenience. In this situation, it is critical to consider a broad range of unique evaluation criteria that characterize various cloud services offered by numerous CSPs.

Although there are four cloud deployment types, based on the scope of this study, the company has the option to either establish a private cloud in-house or outsource it to a public cloud. IBM defined a private cloud as a cloud computing environment where a single customer has exclusive utilization of all hardware and software tools. In a private cloud, the user owns and manages the hardware and may define the precise functions of each component. Companies choose private clouds to meet regulatory compliance requirements or because they have a working environment that involves confidential information, personal identifiable information (PII), intellectual property, and other sensitive data (IBM, n.d.). On the other hand, Microsoft Azure defined public cloud as computing services made available to users over the public internet by third-party providers.

Taking into account the features and interests of the retail industry, it is clear that the industry prioritizes aspects like cheap operating costs, dependability, and the convenience of working across various locations rather than elements like handling sensitive data. A public cloud strategy becomes a more practical choice for retail businesses in light of these factors. The benefits of public cloud solutions are numerous and well-suited to the requirements of the retail industry. First, public cloud providers can use economies of scale to offer affordable solutions, enabling retailers to reduce their initial expenses and scale resources per demand (Dave, Shishodia, 2014). Retail companies wanting to save costs and get an edge over their competitors can notably benefit from this cost-effectiveness. Secondly, the ease of use of public cloud solutions enables retailers to run their business smoothly across numerous locations. Retailers can implement and manage their analytics stack fast and effectively, regardless of geographic limitations, thanks to the scalability and accessibility of the public cloud (LaPointe et al., 2014). Lastly, the dependability and durability of public cloud infrastructure guarantee consistent and continuing access to vital applications and data, ensuring less downtime and offering a solid foundation for retail operations.

2.2 On-Premises vs Cloud Solutions: How to Make the Right Choice

When choosing whether to implement their analytics stack on-premises or in the cloud, FMCG retail firms must carefully consider the following factors in addition to their unique requirements, budgetary constraints, and growth objectives.

1. Type and amount of data to be transferred
2. Flexibility and scaling options
3. Data privacy and data security
4. Cost
5. Mobility

2.2.1 Type and Amount of Data Transferred

The increase in structured, semi-structured, and unstructured data types (such as JSON and logs) coming from SFA applications, APIs, and e-commerce can be overwhelming; hence, it is important to choose a platform that can store all forms of data. Sales Representatives have direct engagement

4

with the trade and are hence a major source of sales data, competition insights, and trade feedback for the company. The sales team captures data using a mobile application (sales force automation) that automates and optimizes sales engagement, which will capture the necessary data on the field and then be synchronized with a distributor management system (DMS), an integrated platform for inventory and order management.

Data collected from online retail sites (e-commerce) are mainly unstructured and are about products, prices, customers, and sales performance. The amount of product data collected on e-commerce sites includes product categories, customer reviews, and supplier information. These data points are used by businesses to learn more about the products that customers commonly search for, view, buy, and mix with other products. Data about online shoppers and their buying behavior, which is made available by cookies, enables e-commerce businesses to analyze consumer interest, preferences, shopping behaviors, purchasing trends, and brand loyalty.

The data generated from multiple sources in the trade needs to be analyzed to provide real-time insights that will aid in understanding customer needs, planning innovation, and staying ahead of the competition. These involve a huge amount of structured, semi-structured, and unstructured data that can be mined to uncover hidden patterns and insights (Balachandran, Prasad, 2017).

The types of data that will be captured includes

1. Quantitative data: the data that can be measured is useful for analyzing trends across data sets and for providing answers to the "what" and "how" questions. (Goertzen, 2017). These data include
   a. Categorical nominal: these are labeled or named data generated during outlet mapping exercise with data captured by SFA, and transferred to a central cloud database called distributor management system. The data captured in this category are the name of retailers, names of outlets, and product names pre-loaded in the inventory master. In e-commerce, categorical nominal data include product data and customer data.
   b. Categorical ordinal: Categorical ordinal data is generated during outlet mapping and grading exercises, ranking outlets based on attributes such as sales volume, consumer footfall, or engagement opportunities. This helps retail companies target resources at specific grading levels. Outlets are graded as A, B, C, D, and E based on relevance to the ranking criteria. This helps retailers provide targeted services and answer questions about physical outlet coverage, such as the category of outlets to cover, the criteria for direct coverage, whether to visit all outlets or only a subset, the skill and resources needed for coverage, different approaches based on grading, competition, and staying ahead of competitors (Marie, n.d.).
   c. Categorical binary: The data presented here is classified into one of two categories, such as Yes or No. Sales representative attendance management and successful sales calls can be selected as Yes or No. Since this data will be produced at many places, SFA that

5

is integrated with the distributor management system must be used to capture it. The ability to indicate whether a customer made a purchase or not is also applicable to e-commerce.

d. Discrete and continuous data are essential in the retail industry for the analysis of various aspects of sales. Discrete data are numeric and non-negative integers, while continuous data are values within a range with decimal points. These data types help in capturing the total quantity sold in cases, total net invoice value, average line per invoice, average drop size per outlet, number of productive calls, effective coverage (ECO), and inventory data. Continuous data, on the other hand, is values within a range that often carry decimal points. These data types are crucial for understanding the sales landscape and identifying areas for improvement.

e. Qualitative data in retail or market intelligence guides the application of data-driven strategies for tangible and measurable results. It aids in developing a thorough understanding of consumer needs and behavior patterns. In the physical outlet channel, the data are collected from the field using SFA devices to capture feedback, merchandising activities, and competition activities, including emerging product threats. In e-commerce, qualitative data help measure the specific prevalence of characteristics or attributes in customers, buyers, or internet visitors. One example of qualitative data is using surveys and consumer reviews to get feedback. The types of qualitative data include binary data, nominal data, and ordinal data.

These data types are not highly confidential but largely require real-time processing; hence, a cloud solution is better suited for the analytics stack deployment than on-premises.

2.2.2 Flexibility & Scaling Options

Flexibility and scalability often refer to a system's capacity to adapt to possible future modifications to its requirements. Cloud solutions are typically more scalable, allowing the company to easily increase or decrease resources based on demand. Software specifications can change over time; therefore, flexibility should be seen from the standpoint of the current specification while bearing in mind that it will likely change at some point in the distant or immediate future. A critical difficulty with the on-premises strategy will be utilization, as the needed resource capacity during use may be below or beyond the capacity indicated during system planning, leading to over- or under-utilization (Juhasz, 2020). Cloud technologies are characterized by flexible scalability and enable an organization to do more than scale up or down, as they allow the integration of a cloud footprint across the organization.

The scaling features of cloud services allow the retail company to meet expansion needs without making costly adjustments to the current IT infrastructure in the case of on-premises. Data centers can easily and swiftly adapt their resources to suit changing business requirements. The expansion of a business globally and the shift to remote employment following the COVID-19 epidemic are examples of the benefits of cloud scalability (Hayward, 2022). The cloud can support thousands of users and tens of thousands of rows of data, promoting collaboration across different retail touch points and business growth.

2.2.3 Data Privacy & Data Security

Data security and privacy are essential considerations when building an analytics stack in FMCG retail. Compliance with data protection requirements is crucial for the management, handling, and storage of data created at various points of sale. On-premises versus cloud security decisions are one of the most important things that businesses must consider in the face of the surge in cyberattacks. Cloud solutions can offer robust encryption, access controls, and compliance certifications to protect data during transfer and storage. On-premises is ideal for companies that need stricter cybersecurity policies; however, cloud services provide a higher security standard as it lessens the chance of on-site security threats (Hayward, 2022). An example is Amazon Macie, which uses machine learning to discover and protect sensitive data in AWS (AWS, n.d.). Cloud solutions allow data generated at retail to be regularly backed up in multiple locations and minimize downtime because data can be quickly restored from backup in the cloud rather than on-premises.

Other factors to consider in selecting a deployment mode are costs and mobility. This is about evaluating the cost implications of on-premises infrastructure investments and maintenance versus the pay-as-you-go model of cloud solutions, considering scalability and long-term cost efficiency. The mobility factor of cloud solutions enables the use of mobile devices for data access and analysis for improved agility, empowers field teams, and facilitates quick decisions in a fast-paced retail environment.

2.3 Change Management Factors in the Analytics Project

A change management strategy must be in place to overcome cultural, procedural, and decisional barriers when switching from a traditional method to a data-driven decision-making approach (Dykes, 2022). It is essential to involve important stakeholders early on in the analytics project, explain its aims, benefits, and purpose, and involve them in decision-making. The change management plan should prepare the company for the constant flow of insights that could change how they conduct business. The following five steps are required to achieve the transformation from the traditional model to cloud services (Dehmer, Niemann, 2018).

1. Current state analysis
2. To-Be analysis and goal setting
3. Best practices and potentials
4. Digital fit
5. Implementation

The first step is to analyze the current situation of the firm, its value chain, and its stakeholders to decide which aspects of the business can benefit from analytics and which cannot. The next step (the to-be analysis) sets the direction for the business by defining the desired outcomes of the transformation. The to-be analysis should clearly describe the future state of the business process. The third step involves adopting best practices that suit the company's capabilities and goals. The fourth step compares the advantages and disadvantages of different deployment options (on-premise or cloud) based on business needs, processes, and market conditions. The final step is to implement the selected model with the help of change management specialists and IT service providers.

2.4 Components of the Analytics Stack

The components of an analytics stack used to create data analytics systems that integrate, gather, process, model, and present data from many data sources include a data collection component, data warehouse, data processing, business intelligence, and visualization component (Martinez, 2022). The purpose of integrating these tools is to produce reliable data that can be utilized to support company operations.

2.4.1 Data Collection Component

There are many data sources across the omnichannel in the retail industry, including application databases (e-commerce), third-party applications (e.g., CRM), and data generated from Sales Force Automation devices. Secondary sales are recorded by SFA devices in the traditional brick-and-mortar channel, and the data produced is sent to the data warehouse. Cloud solutions for data collection are better suited for FMCG retail analytics as the data sources are in different channels, which is not ideal for on-premises, a deployment mode characterized by having sources within the organization's infrastructure. E-commerce stores may store data on when and what was purchased by employing cookies to track user activity patterns, such as which pages users visit and whether or not they abandon shopping carts after purchasing items. Making connections between various events and combining the connections into deeper patterns is required because these massive data streams are unusable in their unprocessed state.

Numerous tools may help gather the raw data from these multiple sources, clean it up, and carry out the necessary processing to get the data ready for placement into a data repository. The first option is to use the Extract & Load process, which entails writing code to extract data from various sources and load it into the target data warehouse. An example of this would be a SQL script set to run every morning, but the cost of maintaining this script may outweigh the advantages over time, so a data loading tool is advised (Nguyen, Pham, Chin, 2020). Data loading tools, or ETL tools, are systems permitting various input or output databases, multi-dimensional designs, the development of surrogate keys, a range of transformation techniques, and native database access (Pall, Khaira, 2013). They contain features like monitoring, scheduling, bulk loading, and incremental aggregation, in addition to reducing the cost of creating and maintaining complex routines. There are numerous data loading tools available in both free and paid versions, allowing faster data sharing between businesses and channels. The data generated at retail are both structured and unstructured; hence, the company can consider integration solutions like Pentaho, Salesforce Connect, Mulesoft, Scribe Software, Numerator Insights, and Stibo Systems (King, 2018).

The extract, transform, and load capabilities required to integrate a wide range of data inputs, such as relational databases, business applications, files, and big data, are provided by the Pentaho Data Integration platform (Sherman, 2016). Pentaho allows retailers to create intelligent supply chains, divide markets into segments, comprehend client purchasing patterns, adopt market-driven pricing and promotions, keep an eye on operations, and ensure field executions and corporate strategy are consistent.

Salesforce Connect is a platform that allows users to search, read, and edit data stored in numerous external sources; it also assists with continual and on-demand information retrieval (Samuel et al., 2021).

Mulesoft is a solution that can connect marketing, POS, and ERP systems to create a 360-degree view of the customer and integrate the consumer experience across in-store, web, and mobile platforms for better service and merchandising decisions (King, 2018).

A retail firm can use the cost-effective, no-coding solutions provided by Scribe Software Corporation as a tool for integrating almost any application, data source, or Software as a Service (SaaS) platform.

The Master Data Management solution from Stibo Systems enables retail companies to benefit from the creation of a centralized database of clean, reliable, and consistent product information, which facilitates multichannel retailing and synchronizes both internal and external systems (King, 2018). Retailers can also run timely and targeted deals thanks to the platform.

2.4.2 Data Warehouse, Data Lake, and Data Platform

The retail organization has the choice of selecting between an on-premises data warehouse and a cloud-based data platform. On-premises warehousing requires the business to buy, deploy, and maintain all hardware and software, in contrast to cloud warehousing, which has no physical infrastructure. As shown in Figure 2, a data warehouse uses ETL to combine data from several sources, acting as the organization's "single source of truth" that decision-makers can trust (Potineni, 2017). Decision makers often employ Online Analytical Processing tools (OLAP), query and reporting tools, and data mining tools to extract business insights from data warehouses, and this is a key component of data-driven decision-making support systems (Zhijuan, Hongchang, Xuefang, 2012). Insights are obtained from dashboards and report to gain inventory analysis and sales performance by product and by the customer, which aids in offering solutions to problems with choosing profitable pricing, having the proper amount of inventory, launching new products, and providing value.

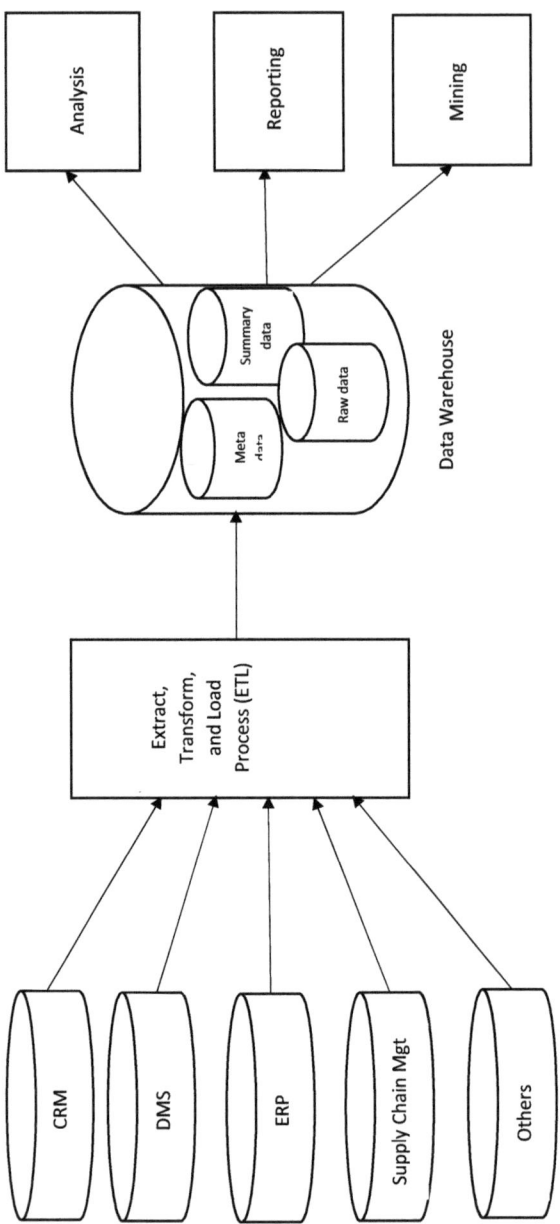

Figure 2: A Data Warehouse (Nambiar, Mundra, 2022).

The two things considered while constructing a data warehouse are operational data sources and user requirements. Operational data sources include numerous databases and systems that house the raw data required for the data warehouse, such as CRM systems, ERP systems, and other operational systems where data is generated. On the other hand, the demands and expectations of the end users who will use the data warehouse for reporting, analysis, and decision-making are referred to as user requirements. The data needed by the retail business should first be determined to meet the demands of the organization, instead of being restricted by the data stored in operational databases.

The three stages in a typical data warehouse design for on-premises are business process analysis, the logical phase, and the physical implementation phase. (Kokaev, 2014).

1. Analysis of Business Processes: The typical business processes of a retail business include secondary sales, purchasing, inventory management, and customer relationship management. The reporting and analysis requirements for each business process are gathered through written documentation once the process has been established and detailed, as explained below:
   a. The reporting and analysis requirements for secondary sales are to analyze sales by retailers, products, salesmen, and outlets. Secondary sales involve selling out, keeping track of transactions, accepting payments from clients, billing, delivering requested goods to clients, managing returns, and responding to customer inquiries.
   b. The reporting and analytical requirements for purchasing include forecasting consumer demand, tracking delivery schedules, and identifying popular and profitable products. The purchasing process involves creating successful product lines that offer customers a variety of products that reflect current trends. The primary tasks associated with the purchasing workflow include selecting which product lines to stock, figuring out how much of each product to order, adding or removing product ranges, interacting with suppliers, and managing delivery schedules.
   c. The reporting and analytical requirements for inventory management include identifying instances of overstocks and understocks, tracking inventory performance, assessing inventory correctness, and ensuring the achievement of reporting and analytical standards. Receiving products, keeping them available for sale, and guaranteeing inventory accuracy are all parts of inventory management.
   d. The reporting and analytical requirements for customer relationship management include mapping out target customers and maintaining all data, including transaction histories.
2. The logical phase: an iterative method is adopted to build a dimensional data model that reflects the specified workflows and satisfies the reporting and analysis needs of the retail company after gathering reporting and analytical requirements and defining business processes (Habte, Ouazzane, Patel, 2017). The logical architecture allows for rapid and

simple responses to business queries by using fact and dimension tables to structure data. A set of informative features in dimension tables defines the context of facts, whereas fact tables record performance metrics produced by business activity or events. According to Oracle Database, unique identifiers should be added to tables to guarantee the consistency of data and distinguish between the same item when it appears in multiple places (Potineni, 2017). During the logical phase, techniques like the third-normal form (3NF), star or snowflake schemas, and hybrid schemas are used to develop the dimensional data model and data warehouse schema, a group of database objects that includes tables, views, indexes, and synonyms (Potineni, 2017). In modeling the retail business process, the fact tables will include secondary sales to physical outlet locations, online orders, accumulating online orders, purchase orders, periodic stock levels, stock taking, and a summary of key performance indexes. The dimensions consist of products, product categories, brand information, customers, dates, outlets, transaction types, payment types, trade promotions, sales team members, warehouse locations, and means of delivery.

3. Physical implementation: The information obtained during the logical design phase is transformed into a representation of the physical database structure during the physical design process, and the design choices are mostly influenced by issues of query performance and database upkeep (Potineni, 2017).

However, rather than engaging in the three cumbersome stages above and maintaining a large IT development team, the retail company can focus more on its business by adopting the cloud-based integration of data warehouses and data lakes. The multichannel retail company generates a variety of data types, such as structured, semi-structured, and unstructured. Traditional data warehouses, however, are not friendly with the last two data types and are unable to handle the large data volumes associated with real-time streaming and increased data velocity; hence, data lakes are required to address these challenges (Zburivsky, Partner, 2022). The argument for a data lake is based on the enormous growth in variety, volume, and velocity of modern analytic data, as well as the limitations of traditional data warehouses to accommodate these increases and the challenge of cost-effectively handling the variety of data produced in omnichannel retail. Data lakes are central storage repositories that allow users to store unstructured, semi-structured, or structured data in its original format at scale, with the functionality of visualizations or dashboards from big data analysis, machine learning, and real-time analytics to make better business decisions (Nambiar, Mundra, 2022).

Cloud service providers create a cloud-native platform for retail companies adopting cloud-based solutions that is cost-effectively able to ingest, integrate, transform, and manage an almost infinite amount of data of any type (Zburivsky, Partner, 2022). The platform enables the retail company to facilitate analytics outcomes and address issues related to data volume, velocity, and variety. Both a data warehouse and a data lake have distinct and important roles to play in the architecture of a modern analytics platform; however, using a cloud data warehouse and a data lake together allows for greater utilization of the cloud's modularity, flexibility, and elasticity to support the needs of different use cases for the retail company. Platform as a Service (PaaS) for data warehouses and data lakes is becoming more prevalent in the cloud, making it possible for data lake design to advance past Hadoop's constraints and to produce a combined data lake and data warehouse platform that was much more advanced than anything that could be produced on-premises.

A solution that integrates the functionalities of the different storage concepts will be better for the analytics project to be cost-effective and modern, hence a data platform. A data platform is an integrated solution that integrates the features of a data lake, data warehouse, data hub, and components of a business intelligence (BI) platform into one tool, resulting in a much more manageable end product. According to a 2021 survey by the Customer Data Platform Institute, 63% of marketers use data platforms for personalized online advertisement and mapping out customers; hence, a retail company that wants to stay ahead of the competition must adopt a modern centralized data platform that is capable of making data actionable, interpreting customer needs, providing insights about customer behavior, and predicting success (CDP, 2022). Regardless of the type of data received, the goal of a data platform is to ingest, store, analyze, and make data available for analysis in the most profitable manner feasible.

Cost and performance are the two factors considered by businesses to choose their cloud data storage provider. A company might require data storage with better configuration, hence will select a cloud storage provider based on performance. The flowchart in Figure 3 serves as a guide for choosing a cloud storage vendor, and it shows the computation for performance ranking on the right and the procedure for cost ranking on the left (Mateen et al., 2021).

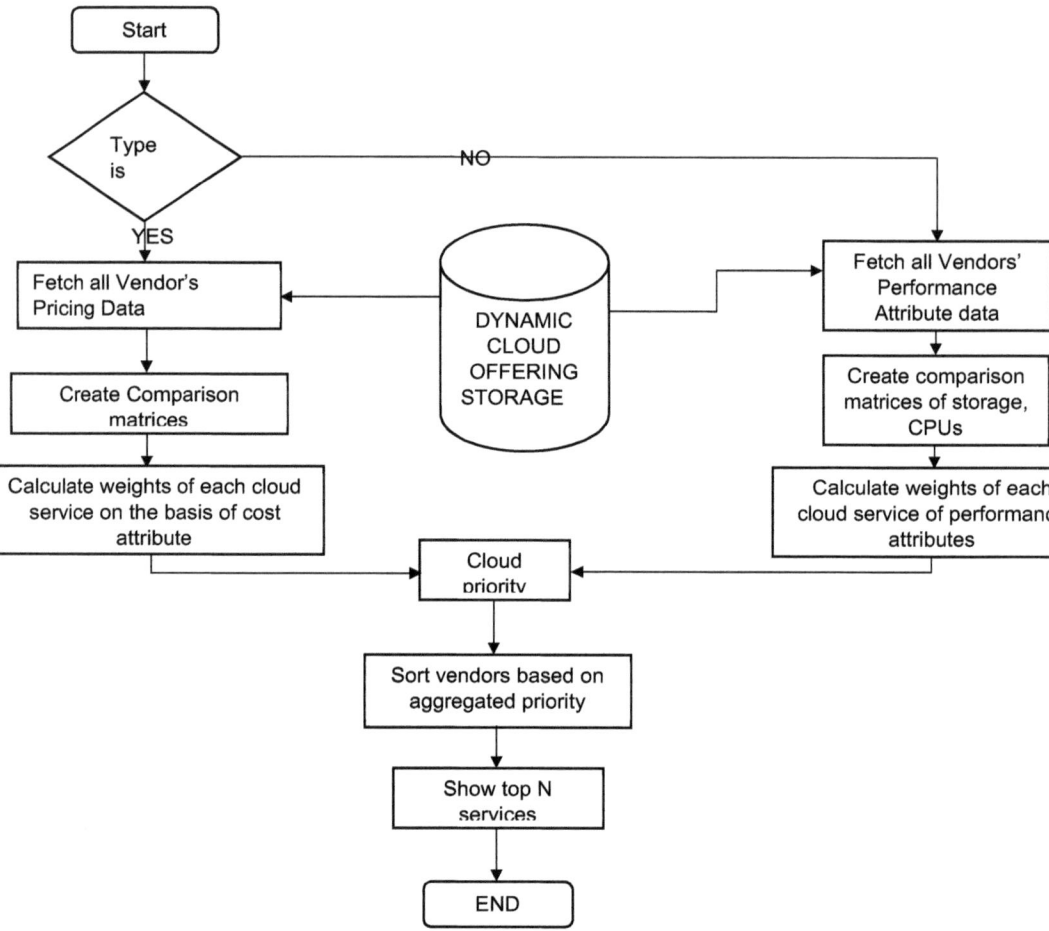

Figure 3: Flow Chart for Selecting a Cloud Storage Provider (Mateen et al., 2021).

The most suitable cloud storage provider should balance compute speed, price, scalability, security, and dependable operation. Vendors have different pricing policies. Pay-as-you-go (PAYG), tiered pricing, and committed use discounts for long-term contracts are a few prevalent pricing structures. Pay-as-you-go (PAYG) pricing models require users to pay for what they use, whereas tiered pricing allows clients a range of costs based on specific capabilities, advantages, or services.

Evaluate vendor performance attributes such as uptime and reliability, network speed, data center locations, scalability, security measures, customer support, and performance benchmarks. Thorough research and comparison are essential to making an informed decision.

Multi-Criteria Decision Making (MCDM) method, also known as Analytic Hierarchy Process (AHP), can be used to calculate the weights of each cloud service based on cost and performance attributes (Alhubaishy, Aljuhani, 2023). For example, when applying AHP method, the first step is to build a hierarchical model for cloud service selection of alternatives A, B, C, and D using cost and performance criteria (Bommannavar et al., 2021). The next step is to assign importance weights to each criterion (Cost and Performance) based on their relative importance in the cloud service selection process, using a scale from 1 to 9, where 1 indicates equal importance, and 9 indicates extremely high importance.

The next step is to create pairwise comparison matrices for each criterion (Cost and Performance) and calculate the eigenvectors, where each element represents the relative importance of alternatives concerning that criterion. Next is to conduct a consistency check by defining the consistency index and consistency ratio, as well as the weighted scores needed for ranking the alternative cloud services. The service alternative with the highest weighted score is the most favorable choice when considering both Cost and Performance criteria with the provided importance weights.

2.4.3 Data Processing and Analysis

For both structured (e.g., sales transactions) and unstructured data (e.g., customer reviews) to be transformed into insights that can be used to make strategic decisions, improve business operations, and improve customer experiences, a retail company's analytics stack must include a data processing and analytics component. Cloud-based data integration and transformation services offer scalability and flexibility for handling large volumes of retail data. This may entail the use of data querying tools like SQL, data transformation frameworks like Apache Spark or Apache Beam, and statistical analysis programs like R or Python for advanced analytics and machine learning. There are many tools; however, getting input from stakeholders, such as business users, managers, and executives, to understand their needs, issues, and suggestions for improvement is one approach to staying current with the newest developments in analytics technologies and taking advantage of the best-suited opportunities.

A retail firm can improve decision-making, operational efficiency, return on investment, customer experience, and competitive advantage by integrating advanced analytics and machine learning into its analytics stack (Fogarty, 2019). Sales managers can use predictive sales analytics to estimate new insights and make better-informed decisions on customer segmentation, recommender systems, and demand forecasting (Habel et al., 2023). Organizations may reliably predict future demand patterns, optimize inventory levels, and enhance supply chain management by examining historical sales data, market trends, seasonality, promotional activity, and external factors. Machine learning algorithms can evaluate consumer data, including purchase history, demographic data, and online activity, to discover customer segments with similar attributes. This aids in targeted promotions to increase customer engagement and loyalty.

2.4.4 Business Intelligence and Visualization Component

The business intelligence and visualization component of an analytics stack comprises business intelligence (BI) systems and representations like reports and dashboards. This component involves a combination of tools, technologies, and methodologies that facilitate data exploration, reporting, and data-driven decision-making. Users of this component can create analytical models that help the retail company understand its historical data, predict future outcomes, and make decisions about how to modify future operations. BI and data visualization tools make it simple to comprehend and work with data, and users can create visualizations and leverage capabilities in BI software like Tableau, Qlik Sense, ThoughtSpot, Looker, and Microsoft Power BI to make data-driven business choices. There are several visualization tools and the choice can be dependent on users need and other factors as shown in Table 1.

Table 1: Comparison of Business Intelligence Tools (Petrossian, 2022).

	Power BI	Tableau	Qlik Sense	ThoughtSpot	Looker	Data Studio
Full-featured free version	Yes	Separate tool	Separate tool	No	No	Yes
Development environment	Desktop	Desktop	Web browser	Implementation	Cloud	Cloud
R and Python Supported	Yes	Yes	Yes	R Only	Yes	Python Only
Dynamic cross-filtering	Yes	Yes	Yes	No	No	Yes
AI-enabled analytics	Yes	Yes	Yes	Yes	No	No
Data Prep tools	Yes	Separate tool	Separate tool	Yes	No	Separate tool
Data Modeling Tools	Yes	Separate tool	Yes	Yes	Yes	No
Preferred Data Model	Star-schema	Flat	Snowflake	Star-schema	Flat	Star-schema/ snowflake
Database Independent	Yes	Yes	Yes	Yes	No	Yes
Built in Row level Security	Yes	Yes	Yes	No	No	Yes

Third-party Data Model Access	Yes	No	No	No	No	No
Embedded Analytics	Yes	Yes	Yes	Yes	Yes	No

It is important to take into account aspects like usability, data integration abilities, scalability, real-time analytics, and total cost of ownership when choosing a BI solution for an FMCG retail organization. A thorough analysis of the business's analytics needs, current IT setup, and projected future growth will aid in making an informed decision. Before making a final decision, it is recommended to run tests and proof-of-concepts using the selected tools to determine how well they match the demands of the firm.

3.1 Conclusion

In conclusion, it is important to carefully weigh the advantages and disadvantages of deploying an analytics stack for a retail organization on-premises or in the cloud. Greater control over data and infrastructure are provided by on-premises implementation, which also ensures adherence to strict data security and privacy laws. Organizations with specific performance requirements can use it since it gives the corporation the opportunity to fine-tune hardware combinations. On-premises deployment, however, necessitates significant up-front investments in hardware and IT personnel, which may ultimately limit scalability and agility.

The scalability, flexibility, and cost-effectiveness of cloud-based analytics systems, however, are unmatched. By utilizing the cloud, retail businesses may obtain computing resources on demand, enabling quick deployment and scalability without major capital expenditures. Additionally, real-time data analysis made possible by cloud-based analytics offers quicker decision-making and the capacity to adjust to changing market conditions. To guarantee data protection and uphold client confidence, issues with data security, compliance, and reliance on third-party service providers must be resolved.

Building an analytics stack is not a one-size-fits-all approach; hence, it should align with the specific needs and goals of the company. Customers interact with retail companies or buy company products in a variety of ways utilizing a variety of platforms, including social media, e-commerce, online chat, and from physical stores. These engagements generate both structured and unstructured data, which comes from a variety of sources and is of diverse quality and volume. Combining all of these touchpoints into a single customer view will make the business achieve a wide range of better business outcomes which includes improved customer satisfaction, personalized marketing, dynamic pricing, lower churn, better cross-selling, edging competition, and many more.

The particular requirements and priorities of the retail organization ultimately determine whether the analytics stack should be deployed on-premises or in the cloud. While cloud solutions offer agility and scalability for businesses looking to stay competitive in a fast-paced, data-driven sector, on-premises solutions may be better ideal for enterprises wanting enhanced data control and compliance. The winning strategy is to cease being a technology laggard and implement a cloud-based integrated analytics stack for a data-driven omnichannel decision-making approach in this fiercely competitive industry for the company to be ahead of the competition and remain relevant.

3.2 Recommendations and Insights

The following are some insights and recommendations for retail businesses that want to leverage the power of data analytics stack solution.

1. Maintain a 360-degree view of each customer by collecting and integrating data from various sources, such as omnichannel sales transactions, loyalty programs, and social media.
2. Improve customer service by extracting insights from unstructured data such as voice conversations, emails, and social media postings using sentiment analysis, natural language processing, and text mining.
3. Use predictive analytics to forecast demand, prevent stock-outs, reduce waste, and optimize resources.
4. Use dynamic pricing algorithms to adjust prices in real-time based on market trends, customer demand, inventory levels, and competitor strategies.

Bibliography

Abdul Mateen, Seung Yeob Nam, Muhammad Ali Haider, Abdul Hanan (2021). A Dynamic Decision Support System for Selection of Cloud Storage Provider. Applied Sciences 11, no. 23: 11296. https://doi.org/10.3390/app112311296

Al Wedell, Dale Hempeck (1987). Sales Force Automation – Here and Now. Journal of Personal Selling and Sales Management, 7(2), 11–16.

Alhubaishy, A., & Aljuhani, A. (2023). A Load-Fairness Prioritization-Based Matching Technique for Cloud Task Scheduling and Resource Allocation. Computer Systems Science & Engineering, 46(1), 2461–2481. https://doi-org.pxz.iubh.de:8443/10.32604/csse.2023.032217

Amanpartap Singh Pall, Jaiteg Singh Khaira (2013). A Comparative Review of Extraction, Transformation and Loading Tools. Database Systems Journal, issue 2, pages 42-51

Athira Nambiar, Divyansh Mundra (2022). An Overview of Data Warehouse and Data Lake in Modern Enterprise Data Management. Big Data and Cognitive Computing. https://doi.org/10.3390/bdcc6040132

AWS (n.d.). What Is Amazon Macie? - Amazon Macie. https://docs.aws.amazon.com/macie/latest/user/what-is-macie.html

Bala M. Balachandran, Shivika Prasad (2017). Challenges and Benefits of Deploying Big Data Analytics in the Cloud for Business Intelligence, Procedia Computer Science, Volume 112, 2017, Pages 1112-1122, ISSN 1877-0509, https://doi.org/10.1016/j.procs.2017.08.138.

Bommannavar, P. A., Shah, A., Singh, A., & R, K. (2021). Analyzing Performance Parameters for Cloud Service Selection using AHP. 2021 6th International Conference for Convergence in Technology (I2CT), Convergence in Technology (I2CT), 2021 6th International Conference For, 1–7. https://doi-org.pxz.iubh.de:8443/10.1109/I2CT51068.2021.9418148

Brynjolfsson Erik, Hitt Lorin, Kim Heekyung (2011). Strength in Numbers: How Does Data-Driven Decisionmaking Affect Firm Performance? Retrieved from https://www.socialserviceworkforce.org/system/files/resource/files/Data%20Driven%20Deci sions.pdf

CDP (2022, June 15). CDP vs. Data Warehouse: What's Best for Your Business? CDP.com - Leading CDP Industry Resource For Marketing & Sales - News, Analysis And Thought Leadership Content on The CDP Industry. https://cdp.com/articles/cdp-vs-data-warehouse/

Chartio (n.d.). An Overview of an Analytics Data Stack. https://chartio.com/learn/data-warehouses/an-overview-of-an-analytics-data-stack/

Dave, M., & Shishodia, Y. S. (2014). Cloud economics: Vital force in structuring the future of cloud computing. 2014 International Conference on Computing for Sustainable Global Development (INDIACom), Computing for Sustainable Global Development (INDIACom), 2014 International Conference On, 61–66. https://doi-org.pxz.iubh.de:8443/10.1109/IndiaCom.2014.6828022

Dykes, B. (2022, November 29). Why Change Management Skills Are Essential To Data-Driven Success. Forbes. https://www.forbes.com/sites/brentdykes/2022/11/29/why-change-management-skills-are-essential-to-data-driven-success/

Fogarty, D. J. (2019). Issues and Advantages of Advanced Analytics, Machine Learning, and Artificial Intelligence in the Workplace. Emerald Publishing Limited. https://doi-org.pxz.iubh.de:8443/10.1108/978-1-78973-073-920191012

FullStory. (n.d.). Qualitative Data: Examples and How to Use It | FullStory. https://www.fullstory.com/blog/qualitative-data-examples/

Gautam Pal, Gangmin Li, Katie Atkinson (2018). Multi-Agent Big-Data Lambda Architecture Model for E-Commerce Analytics. Doi:10.3390/data3040058.

Habel, J., Alavi, S., & Heinitz, N. (2023). A theory of predictive sales analytics adoption. AMS Review: Official Publication of the Academy of Marketing Science, 13(1–2), 34–54. https://doi-org.pxz.iubh.de:8443/10.1007/s13162-022-00252-0

Habte S., Ouazzane K., Patel P., Patel S. (2017). Generic Data Warehousing for Consumer Electronics Retail Industry. Retrieved from https://core.ac.uk/download/pdf/96599431.pdf

Hagiu Andrei, Wright Julian (2020, January 1). When Data Creates Competitive Advantage. Harvard Business Review. https://hbr.org/2020/01/when-data-creates-competitive-advantage

Hayward, A. (2022, February 2). On-premise vs. Cloud: The Implications On Data Security. Compare the Cloud. https://comparethecloud.net/articles/big-data-articles/data-protection/on-premise-vs-cloud-the-implications-on-data-security/

IBM. (n.d.). What Is Private Cloud? | IBM. https://www.ibm.com/topics/private-cloud

Joanna Dehmer, Jörg Niemann (2018). Value Chain Management Through Cloud-based Platforms. Procedia - Social and Behavioral Sciences 238 (2018) 177 – 181

Juhasz, Z. (2021). Quantitative Cost Comparison of On-premise and Cloud Infrastructure Based EEG Data Processing. Cluster Comput 24, 625–641 https://doi-org.pxz.iubh.de:8443/10.1007/s10586-020-03141-y

Kanade Vijay (2021). Cloud vs. On-Premise Comparison: Key Differences and Similarities. Retrieved from https://www.spiceworks.com/tech/cloud/articles/cloud-vs-on-premise-comparison-key-differences-and-similarities/

KPMG. (2016). *Fast-moving Consumer Goods Sector Report.* Retrieved from https://assets.kpmg/content/dam/kpmg/br/pdf/2016/09/fast-moving-consumer-goods.pdf

Madhu Bala, Dinesh Kumar (2011). Supply Chain Performance Attributes for the Fast-Moving Consumer Goods Industry. *Journal of Transport & Supply Chain Management.* DOI:10.4102/jtscm.v5i1.19

Matthew LaPointe, Lucas Walker, Matthew Nelson, Justin Shananaquet, Xinli Wang (2014). Comparing public and private iaas cloud models. Association for Computing Machinery. https://doi-org.pxz.iubh.de:8443/10.1145/2656434.2656449

Melissa J. Goertzen (2017). Applying Quantitative Methods to E-book Collections. *American Library Association.* https://doi.org/10.5860/ltr.53n4

Microsoft (2022, November 15). Data management in the retail industry - Azure Architecture Center. Data Management in the Retail Industry - Azure Architecture Center | Microsoft Learn. https://learn.microsoft.com/en-us/azure/architecture/industries/retail/retail-data-management-overview

Nguyen Huy, Pham Ha, Chin Cedric (2020). The Analytics Setup Guidebook. Holistics. Retrieved from https://cdn.holistics.io/guidebook/the-analytics-stack-guidebook.pdf

Samuel, N., Banerjee, A., & Reddy, A. (2021, October 22). Salesforce Connect: The Ultimate Guide. Learn | Hevo. https://hevodata.com/learn/salesforce-connect/

Padmaja Potineni (2017). Oracle Database Data Warehousing Guide. Retrieved from https://docs.oracle.com/database/121/DWHSG/toc.htm

Petrossian, G. (2021, May 27). Business Intelligence Tools Comparison Chart - SkyPoint Cloud. SkyPoint Cloud. https://skypointcloud.com/blog/business-intelligence-tools-comparison-chart/

Rick Sherman (2016). An Overview of the Pentaho Data Integration Platform. Retrieved from https://www.techtarget.com/searchdatamanagement/feature/An-overview-of-the-Pentaho-Data-Integration-platform

Marie, R. (n.d.). Retail Outlet Classification in RtM Strategy, an Essential Element or a Complete Waste of Time? Retail Outlet Classification in RtM Strategy, an Essential Element or a Complete Waste of Time? https://supplychain.enchange.com/https/supplychain.enchange.com/retail-outlet-classification-in-rtm-strategy-an-essential-element-or-a-complete-waste-of-time

Kokaev Slava (2014). Business Process Modeling and Analysis for Data Warehouse Design. https://www.slideshare.net/vkokaev/business-process-modeling-and-analysis-for-data-warehouse-design-39728748

Timothy King (2018, April 27). Best Data Integration Vendors, News & Reviews for Big Data, Applications, ETL and Hadoop. https://solutionsreview.com/data-integration/retail-data-integration-4-software-tools-to-consider/

Tomar, A., Kumar, R.R., Gupta, I. (2022). Decision making for cloud service selection: a novel and hybrid MCDM approach. Cluster Comput. https://doi-org.pxz.iubh.de:8443/10.1007/s10586-022-03793-y

Traasdahl Are (2021, October 18). The Modern Consumer Goods Tech Stack: Creating a Data-Ready Foundation. https://consumergoods.com/modern-consumer-goods-tech-stack-creating-a-data-ready-foundation

Wang Zhijuan, Wei Hongchang, Wu Xuefang (2012). A Data Warehouse Design Method. International Conference on Computer Science and Service System, pp. 2063-2066, doi: 10.1109/CSSS.2012.513.

Zawaideh, F. H., Ghanem, W. A. H. M., Yusoff, M. H., Saany, S. I. A., Jusoh, J. A., El-Ebiary, Y. A. B. (2022). The Layers of Cloud Computing Infrastructure and Security Attacking Issues. *Journal of Pharmaceutical Negative Results*, 13, 792–800. https://doi-org.pxz.iubh.de:8443/10.47750/pnr.2022.13.S05.124

Zburivsky Danil, Partner Lynda (2022). Designing Cloud Data Platforms. https://livebook.manning.com/book/designing-cloud-data-platforms/designing-cloud-data-platforms/4